Dear Parent:
Your child's love of reading starts here!

Every child learns to read in a different way and at his or her own speed. Some go back and forth between reading levels and read favorite books again and again. Others read through each level in order. You can help your young reader improve and become more confident by encouraging his or her own interests and abilities. From books your child reads with you to the first books he or she reads alone, there are I Can Read Books for every stage of reading:

SHARED READING
Basic language, word repetition, and whimsical illustrations, ideal for sharing with your emergent reader

BEGINNING READING
Short sentences, familiar words, and simple concepts for children eager to read on their own

READING WITH HELP
Engaging stories, longer sentences, and language play for developing readers

READING ALONE
Complex plots, challenging vocabulary, and high-interest topics for the independent reader

ADVANCED READING
Short paragraphs, chapters, and exciting themes for the perfect bridge to chapter books

I Can Read Books have introduced children to the joy of reading since 1957. Featuring award-winning authors and illustrators and a fabulous cast of beloved characters, I Can Read Books set the standard for beginning readers.

A lifetime of discovery begins with the magical words "I Can Read!"

Visit www.icanread.com for information
on enriching your child's reading experience.

I Can Read Book® is a trademark of HarperCollins Publishers.

Guinness World Records: Remarkable Robots
© 2017 Guinness World Records Limited.
The words GUINNESS WORLD RECORDS and related logos are trademarks of Guinness World Records Limited.
Images on pages 2, 8, 17, 19, 20, 24, 25, 27, 29, 30, 31 © Alamy.
All records and information accurate as of May 1, 2016.
For information address HarperCollins Children's Books, a division of HarperCollins Publishers, 195 Broadway, New York, NY 10007.
www.icanread.com

Library of Congress Control Number: 2016940572
ISBN 978-0-06-234192-1 (trade bdg.) — ISBN 978-0-06-234191-4 (pbk.)
Typography by Erica De Chavez

16 17 18 19 20 SCP 10 9 8 7 6 5 4 3 2 1   ❖   First Edition

I Can Read!™

READING 2 WITH HELP

GUINNESS WORLD RECORDS

GUINNESS WORLD RECORDS®

REMARKABLE ROBOTS

by Delphine Finnegan

Photos supplied by
Guinness World Records

HARPER
An Imprint of HarperCollins Publishers

Robots come in
all different shapes and sizes.
The **largest walking robot**
is 26 feet, 10 inches high
and looks like a dragon!
If you're ever in Germany,
you may see it at a festival.
But don't get too close—
it breathes fire!

Other robots are very small.
The **smallest robot humanoid**
stands only 6 inches high.
It can walk, kick,
and do push-ups!

Some robots act more like animals than humans.

Robodog from the United Kingdom is the **largest robot dog** at 2 feet, 6 inches high.

Cuddly PARO the seal
is the **most therapeutic robot**.
He helps patients relax
when they are in the hospital.

The LumiPuff lives
in a bowl of water.

It looks and acts just like a real fish.

It is the **first wireless-powered**

aquatic toy.

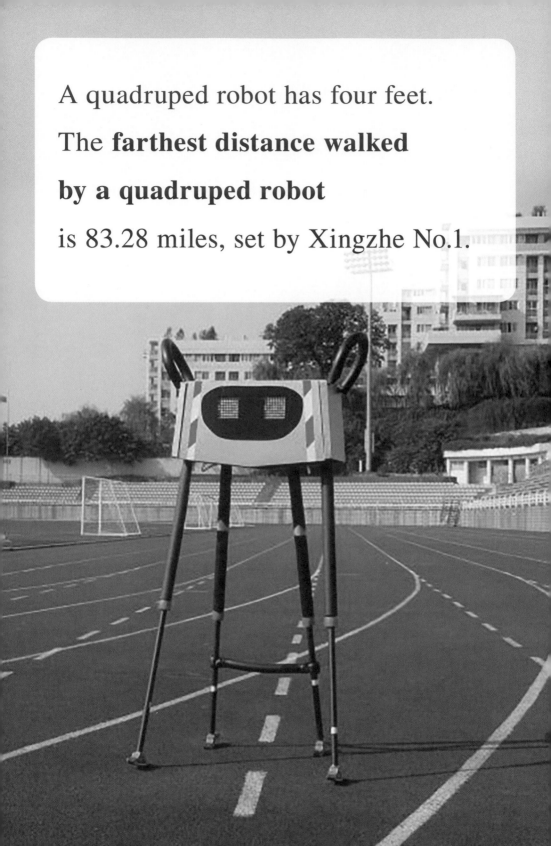

A quadruped robot has four feet. The **farthest distance walked by a quadruped robot** is 83.28 miles, set by Xingzhe No.1.

When an underground tunnel collapsed and flooded in Finland, this remote-controlled (RC) robot inspected the damage.
It traveled 74.56 miles—the **longest tunnel survey by an RC robot**.

And way up high, in 2013,
Kirobo, from Japan, became
the **first companion robot in space**.

Kirobo is a multi-record holder. By speaking with an astronaut on the International Space Station, more than 257 miles above Earth, it became the **highest-altitude robot to have a conversation**.

The **most robots dancing at the same time** is 540. They performed at a festival in China in 2016.

Robots have all sorts of jobs.
In Hong Kong, some
robots work in restaurants!
China's Robot Kitchen was
the **first restaurant**
with robotic waiters.
One robot will take your order,
while another serves your meal.

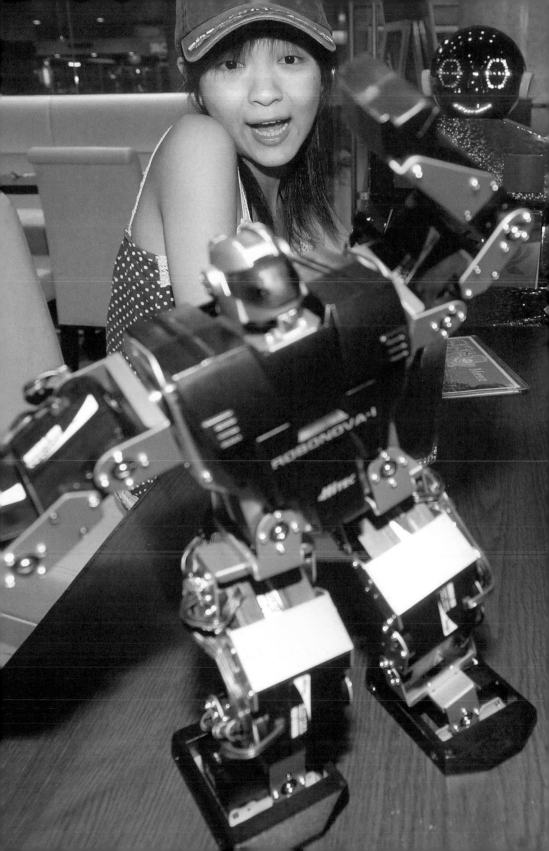

Made in Switzerland, the PUMA robot is the **most widely used industrial robot**. It works in school labs and assembles cars in factories.

Robots work at home, too.

The **first robot babysitter**

has camera eyes and microphone ears.

This means parents can see

what's happening wherever they are.

Some robots even ride camels for a living! The **fastest robot jockey** reached a top speed of 25 miles per hour (mph).

It's not all work, though.

Robots also know how to play.

The Raonic Robot from Japan can fire

tennis balls at 169.6 mph—

that's the **fastest serve by a machine**.

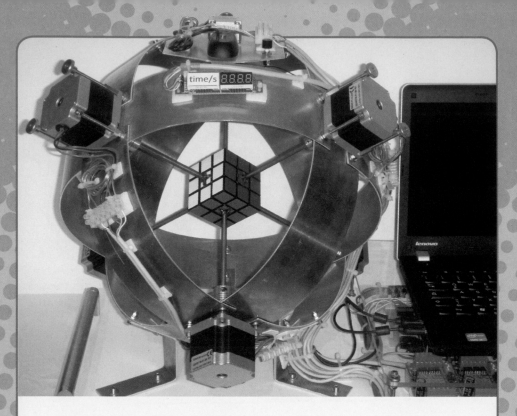

Robots also like to play with toys.

Sub1 from Germany

is the **fastest robot**

to solve a Rubik's Cube.

It finished the puzzle

in just 0.887 seconds!

Made in Vietnam, the **longest-running mechanical spinning top** spun for 24 hours, 35 minutes, and 15 seconds. Good thing robots don't get dizzy!

Some robots have musical talents. The **first robot trumpeter** was built by Toyota in Japan. "Over the Rainbow" is one of the songs it can play.

The American toy Furby

was the **first AI robot toy**.

AI stands for

"artificial intelligence."

It spoke its own language (Furbish)

and a few English words, too.

Flying robots called drones
are really taking off. . . .
The **most drones flying
at the same time** is 100,
set by Intel in Germany.

Robots also have the power
to help save lives.

Atlas, the **most agile humanoid
robot**, walks across uneven ground
and is fitted with sensors.

This droid can work in places
too unsafe for emergency workers.

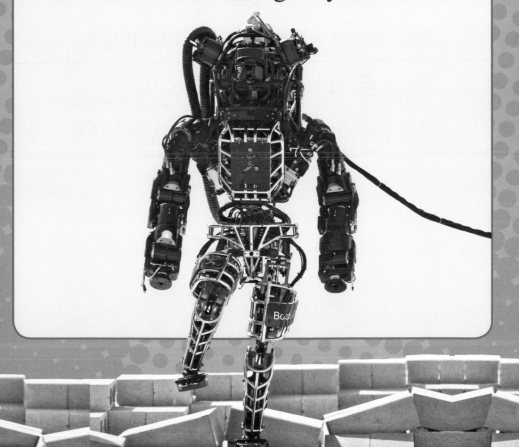

ASIMO, the **fastest-running humanoid robot**,

can move at 5.5 mph.

It performs a range of tasks

and even knows sign language.

It took more than 20 years

for engineers to create ASIMO.

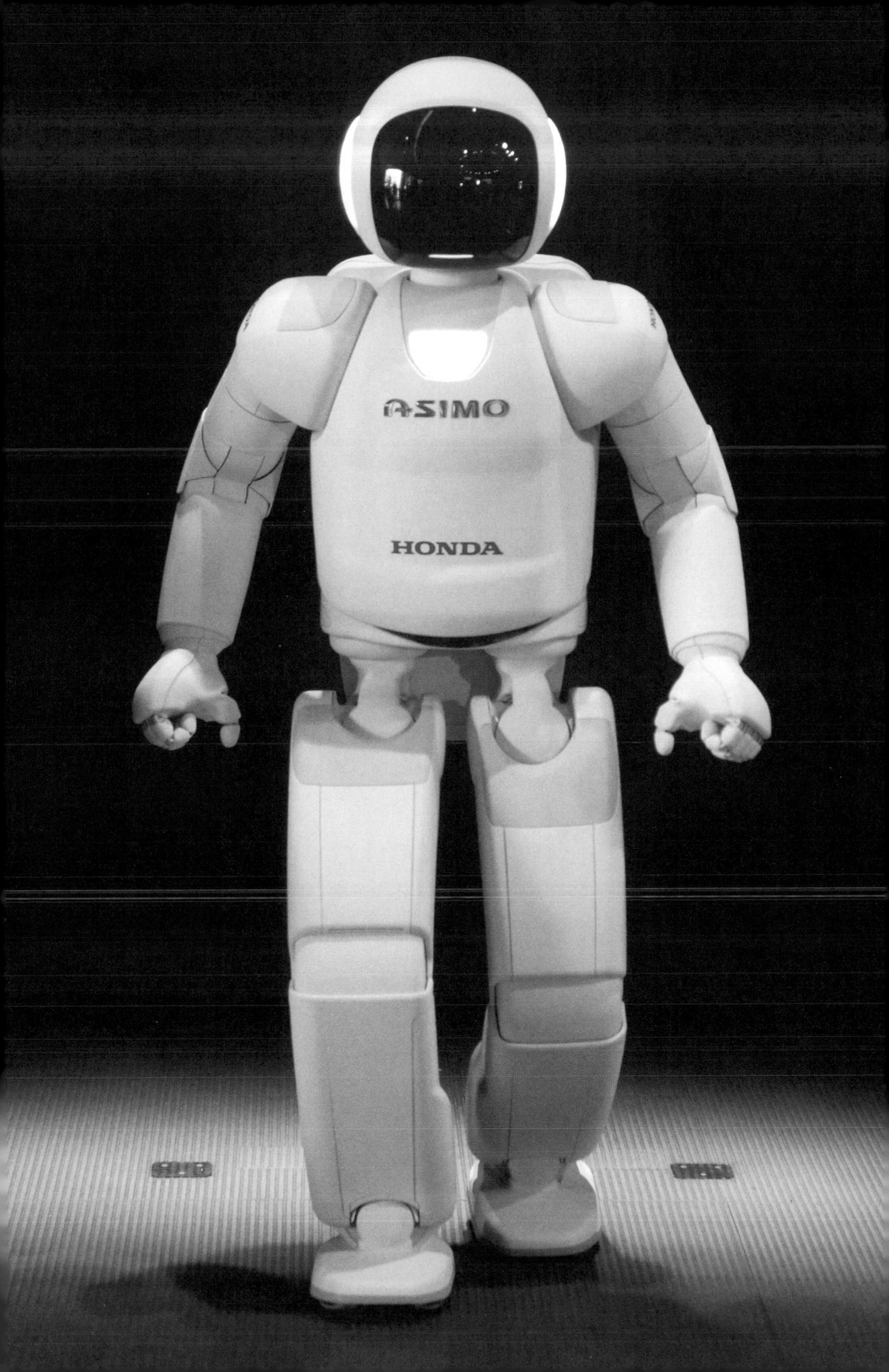
ASIMO
HONDA

One day you may not even be able

to tell the difference

between a human and a robot. . . .

The Geminoid HI-1,

the **first android avatar**,

blinks and fidgets just like us.

Also from Japan, the Geminoid DK is the **most lifelike android**. It can display different emotions and moves just like a real person.

The best way to get to know robots is to study them.

Students in Hong Kong connected 255 four-legged robots on the same day—resulting in the **longest chain of robots**!